THE JOURNEY JOURNAL

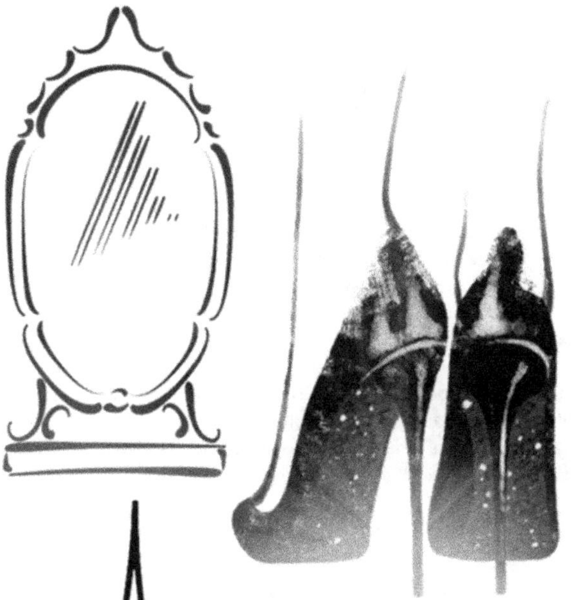

A BRICK ROAD TO A Comeback

Written by: CHRISTYNA WITH A "Y"

A Brick Road To A Comeback
Journey Journal

This Journey Journal is Originally Created by the author with the inspiration of the original motion picture, The Wizard of Oz (Vidor, King, et al. The Wizard of Oz. Metro-Goldwyn-Mayer (MGM), 1939.) Other than names/title references, no parts of the script/screenplay have been used in this body of work.

Book Completion Services Provided by:
TRU Statement Publications—Independent Publishing Made Easy
www.trustatementpublications.com

First Edition: February 2021
Printed in the United States of America
02222021
ISBN: 978-1-948085-54-0

This is a collection of Journal entries I wrote to encourage myself through the darkest period of my life. I wrote my thoughts as if I were taking a trip, having a purposeful adventure that was needed to allow me to release the ME I saw in my dreams. I needed help reconciling me to the parts of myself that I had abandoned while trying to BE someone who was not ME.

I would like to dedicate this work to those who:

Ignited Me

My former husband, who taught me there are levels of love, and in that ignited my desire to take a journey to true love and forgiveness…

Fueled Me

C. Scott Washington, Jr., Morgan Kennedy Washington, and my brother, Patrich “Uncle P” Giles, because you are the kindling that keeps me striving to make an impact on this world; making it a better place for you and your children to dwell.

Inspired Me

The THREE: My Grandmother, Rebecca Hawkins, who went from being a domestic (house keeper in the south) to a business owner in her 50's and didn't officially retire and sell her business until she was in her 80's; my Aunt Ora, the powerhouse who put a family on her shoulders and made sure we all had a better life; and my Mom, Mable the great Adventurer, who without your vision, example, and encouragement I would not be here. Because you loved me out loud, I am able to do so as well.

Loved Me

Everyone needs a Libby; that sister friend who is firm in her word, focused on her intent, and a strong shoulder when you need one. Someone who knows how to pull your chain while stepping on your foot to help you press the gas in your life.

And my... *he who shall not be named.* You breathed life into me by hearing me when I couldn't speak, comforting me when I was numb, and always pushing me to "stand up in my heels" as a whole complete woman. You will never know what your love has meant to me.

Covered Me

The Circle of Sisters, for drenching me in effectual prayer in my attempt to come back to life. Not only did you pray for me, you laughed with me and cried with and for me; sisters both old and new, thank you all.

And My "Companion" Big, for revealing to me my truth of wanting what I want and recognizing it as my calling and purpose, for walking the road to my comeback with me, lifting me in those times I couldn't lift myself, and allowing me to be me.

Carried Me

My Lord and Savior Jesus Christ

And You...

Yes, YOU! The journeyer who I have lovingly called "Bricklayers." It is my intention that this journey unlocks a sense of adventure and ignites the curiosity of your inner self.

Enjoy your journey,

Christyna with a "Y"

Contents

This Journal was birthed out of my attempt to make sense of my life, after having decided I wanted to blow up my life as I knew it and rebuild the life I had dreamed of. While the journey was never straight, in every moment I was always standing on solid ground, with my head clear, and a reminder of the blood that flows through my veins. As I **ReLoaded, ReLearned, and Realized**, I wrote every thought knowing that I was not doing the work for myself, but as a trial run for those who may also be in or entering into a transition of life.

My foundational verse was and will always be Philippians 4:13, which states,

“I can do all things through Christ who strengthens me.”

It reminds me that everything I needed was and is always within me. I just had to go through experiences which allowed me to reach and release the power of Me.

This Journey Journal is a collection of my diary entries, written as I imagined this day when I would be speaking to you — Yes, YOU! I wrote to you before I even met you or thought of you picking up this Journal to go on your own Journey.

It is my intent that this Journey Journal provides you with experiences, questions, and insight that you need to live the life you truly want. My dream is that it illuminates parts of your life's path when you find it dark, lonely, and brickless; that you will use this journal as a light to unlock the answers you have within, to provide you clarity or even a push to acknowledge, release, and move forward.

Remember in the story of the Wizard of Oz, or the Wiz (depending upon your story preference), Dorothy found out that everything she needed was with her all the time. My desire is the same for you.

So, now I say to you, Bon Voyage…

And remember, **Transitions are either TRIALS of Adversity or TRAILS of Adventure.** It's all in where you put your 'I.' Shoot me a line and share which side you found yours on.

Remember, I/***We*** walk with you,

Christyna with a "Y"

Introduction

I spent the past two weeks between 2012 and 2013, maybe like you (especially now in 2020) reflecting on things I did right, what I did wrong, and what I want to improve on in the new year. However, today, I spent a little time thinking about my mother.

It's been 9 years since her transition; so, when I want to feel close to her, I go through all of her jewelry. Today a funny thing happened, her ruby ring kept falling out of the jewelry bag—for no reason. It's a ring I remember she always wore, and I guess because of that I refused to wear it, let alone try it on. As fate would have it, I slipped the ring on and here on this paper is the result of what the experience made me think of.

I thought of the wisdom that poured out of my mom like water and how she was so graceful under such pressure, and in a split second I felt like Dorothy from the Wizard of Oz. The stresses of juggling family, career, and seeking to make a financial comeback has had me feeling like I'm on a proverbial yellow brick road, knowing I'm on the right track and taking the curves that the road throws.

I'm sure your road has also taken some unexpected turns as well. I thought about the courage it takes to stay on the road—ahh...The Lion. Knowing that I may have to

Relearn some things, some old ideas or thoughts I had on various subjects may have to be reexamined. Thoughts on family values, gender roles, and money; what I learned to get here isn't going to carry me through to where I want to go on this leg of the road.

I with my mom's ruby ring (my version of a ruby slipper) am embarking on this leg of the yellow brick road of life with a desire to find my way back home. Join me; maybe you'll find something that helps you find your way back home.

Through these pages, I will be speaking to you on good old kitchen table topics and financial fortitude for your comeback. These three words will always be the thread of each conversation for you, and me too!

Realize — realization according to Webster is bringing into actuality. I believe it is a submission to the thought or reality that something has to change and putting your focus on it making that happen.

ReLearn — learn according to Webster is, come to know or know how. I believe it's the opportunity to know what you thought you knew, this time knowing it correctly.

ReLoad — load according to Webster is, to make ready for firming. I believe reloading is the ability to start over, to redo with the correct foundation.

Let's begin our journey.

Christyna with a "Y"

Have you ever been in the company of someone and started imagining what their life might be like based on their car? Title? Or maybe their representative? Yes, their representative…

Over the course of this week, I have been checking in with friends and was sharing how I was thinking about mom; how I used to envy my mom for her style, her model looks, and awesome abilities as a mom. My mom was the quintessential hot mom. She would pick me up from junior high school, and the teachers and people in general would ask me if she was my sister. It would burn me up!

I wanted so much to be like my mom; she was a tall woman, with a slender model frame, naturally long hair, and a broad smile. She was a high-ranking executive within the federal government system, traveled back and forth to Washington DC, and had power and influence, in the sense of her title. The one thing my mom never did, because of her job classification, was flash. Even though she had the look, power of her position, and the smarts, when you met her, you met her! Unlike what's common today.

Which takes me back to the 'representative.' I live in Los Angeles where there are as many kept men as there are kept women, where you can see someone who drives a Bentley but lives with their mom, or the most well put together woman dripping in designer labels with no bank account. Representatives, come in all forms, job titles, cars, fashions, etc. They are who you have people meet first. Don't get me wrong, representatives are good, they allow us to decide if we want to engage or not, but what if there is nothing beyond the Rep? No depth to the story, just a car, just a title, etc. Do you think you'd be satisfied? I think not. If you're like me, you want your authentic you too be just as strong or bomb as your representative.

Conversations with Christyna

The Authentic You is always going to be more sustainable and interesting than the representative you; so might as well make them one in the same!

I had a conversation with a powerhouse of a man, who had a little stumble on his path where he found brickless parts of his road. In his life, he is the quintessential LION; I mean, he rules his part of the jungle and has the accolades, salary, and influence to prove it. However, on the day he and I had our conversation, he was having a crisis of identity. He decided to abandon the "he" he had been in title and showing up as in the world, and his question to me was, "What do I do now?"

Here's what I shared with him…

> *Mr. What do I do Now?*
>
> *How exciting! You took the leap to bet on you. I know for sure it may have you feeling a little uneasy, but guess what? Now you are the captain of your very own ship, you report to your own board, and you get to discover new areas of yourself.*
>
> *Did you know, as the leader you were never really able to fully engage "The You," you desired to be, because you were the face of the organization. YOU now get to freely use ALL of your powerful skills developed as an executive to take on new endeavors, explore, and develop while you venture into new arenas.*
>
> *Take this time to clarify what and who you NOW want to be seen as. You once shared how overwhelmed you always felt. Breathe, take this time to breathe and remember you are the YOU, you have always been in the equation, and you experienced all of those experiences that got you to where you are.*

> *Remove the pressure of what your title carries TO OTHERS and create a new narrative and standard for you in this new chapter, so when you take that seat with those three letters again, you'll bring a new level of empathy to your power position.*
>
> *Last thing, Mr. What do I do Now?... BE YOU, those letters you rock, you earned over the past 20 yrs. YOU defined them, they did not make you!*

If this is you, and you are feeling a little overwhelmed by the constraints of the life you have and are suffering from a little imposter syndrome of your own, I would invite you to:

1. Remember it was YOU who STARED in everything that has gotten you to where you are and will help you as you are renewing.

2. Be GRATEFUL for ALL experiences that have made you who you are and know you can leverage them to become who you are looking to become.

3. Evaluate your core values. Make sure they are truly what you align with and are skilled in, which will help you meet and achieve your truth.

4. Take the leap, every eagle has to be pushed out of the nest, knowing that the young bird is ready and all they have to do is FLAP, all you have to do is FLEX. Your experience has value.

Journal the Journey

Here's your chance to **ReLoad** (there's the word) and develop your Representative to look more like the you, you're destined to be. Perhaps now's the time to revamp your look, take on a mentor for career development, or get your finances refreshed? In whatever stage you're in, the steps are the same.

With the two majors being:

1. Identify where you are

   and…

2. Question where and who do you want to be.

So, my question to you is, Who's your Rep? and, what are you doing to make the representative you, the Authentic YOU?

____

____

____

____

____

____

____

1 Peter 2:9

1 Peter 2:9

1 Peter 2:9

I once had a manager who used to say, “A lion wakes up in the evening prior to the hunt and asks himself, ‘Who am I going to kill today’?” This made me ask myself the question: ***What is my ROAR—CRY!***

As someone like you who wears many hats in life, mother, sister, friend, businesswoman, domestic engineer, etc., I sometimes find roaring more confused with saying, pick up your clothes, brush your teeth, it’s where you left it yesterday, or stop fighting and go to your room! When I think a little more on the nature of the lion, I see why the lion rules; the lion is the King of the jungle. When the lion roars, all that hears his roar run, for they know it’s on.

A roar maybe your swag, your vibe, or your courage! I remember my Grandfather had a roar. When he was ‘stepping out’ he would look as sharp as a new penny, hit the bottom stair, open the door, and tell my grandmother, “Stepping out!” He was so pumped; knew he looked good, smelled good, and was ready to conquer the day and whatever challenge that stood in his way. Which brings me back to—What's your roar?

As I said, it can be your vibe, swag, or your COURAGE! Perhaps over the past few years, through situations and circumstances beyond your control, your roar has been a little shaky, unrecognizable, or even silenced! Trust me, I know. Two years ago, my roar sounded like that of a hoarse baby cub. It took a sad realization to let me know how I had stumbled off my path and had no clue how to get back; it took Realization to wake me up and make me take action.

Conversations with Christyna

I had a question asked during a planning conversation with a young client who was just starting the accumulation phase of life. The interesting thing was, she was the first in her family to graduate from college and would now be the first to purchase a home. You would think she would be over the moon with excitement, but for some reason she wasn't. In fact, she was full of fear. The more we spoke, the more I understood she didn't want to lose her feeling of acceptance. To be honest, she said she didn't want to have too much, and a man not want her.

Here is what I shared (AFTER I almost broke my phone gripping it so tight) …

Dear Graduate and First-Time homeowner,

Wow, not only do I hear you, I once believed that same thing—until I didn't. I bought my first home when I was 29 and dating. Instead of purchasing the "starter home" I qualified for, I opted for the townhouse, as if to "downgrade" my success and still fit in. The more I tried to dim my light, the more I found myself in situations that required me to shine and level up. It sounds like you are where I was.

I had to make a decision that I was worthy of every accomplishment and could celebrate every level of achievement, even if it was by myself for a while. I had to be my own Shero, and I invite you to do so as well, for you have nothing but a future ahead.

If you start dimming now, for the sake of others, what will you look like when you reach your highest heights? My guess is, hunched over from always trying to lower yourself… LIVE out loud and if they don't like it, they'll leave and you would still have Become, Seen, and ACCOMPLISH all sorts of new things.

If you too suffer from being influenced by people who don't have your best interest, or if you live your life FOR OTHERS, I invite you to simply try this:

1. Get to the real truth; what are you really afraid of?

2. Adopt the mindset that you are the liberator OR the prisoner, but you cannot be both.

3. Find some mentors or a like-minded, ambitious circle of people to interact with from time to time like those in Meetup groups or other professional organizations.

4. Breathe, give yourself a chance to stand flat-footed, and take in ALL your success, you might just like the feeling and want to climb higher.

Journal the Journey

I believe the steps I took may help you recover your ROAR—CRY. It works in any area, your relationships, finances, even career, it just takes realization and these ***five steps***:

1. Pinpoint exactly where you are right now in your journey.
2. Discover if course correction is needed.
3. Identify tools or people who can help you rebound.
4. Create a plan; set a start and completion date.
5. Implement the plan; take action.

____

____

____

____

____

____

____

Joshua 1:9

WHAT DOES YOUR ROAR SOUND LIKE?

Joshua 1:9

WHAT DOES YOUR ROAR SOUND LIKE?

Joshua 1:9

The scene closes with Diana Ross being serenaded by the great Lena Horne, who is telling her to believe in herself… for in your heart you'll know! Sometimes the brick road runs thin on bricks. And you have to rely on your instincts, mother wit, or intuition. If you believe the path you're on is correct, just keep on your way, the bricks will reappear.

Often times in our lives, we see areas with thin brick which is a sign to stop and turn around; however, sometimes brickless paths are opportunities for us to create and develop parts of ourselves that may be underutilized. Belief is one of those areas. As a child, I believed I was a *princess.* I would do all the dainty things I thought a princess would do. I would put on mom's heels, one of her nightgowns (for the flow) and cover a wooden spoon in foil as my sector. You couldn't tell me I wasn't a princess; it was those simple items that transformed me and my belief that made it true.

That innocence a child brings, in the way of belief, is what some of us must **ReLearn**. Even now as an adult, I sometimes use those same techniques to transfer myself and my thinking, harnessing a great deal of belief to make things happen in business and in my personal life. I must always believe the outcome is going to be positive, and even though, like Dorothy's travels, there are many twists and turns to come along, I still have to continue the journey.

Today I closed my eyes, click my heels, took a deep breath, and started saying there is no place like home. Home is where those who love you know you, the real you, and except you and it's all good. Home is where the experience of the journey can be implemented for your comeback.

Conversations with Christyna

I was having a conversation with a client; we were planning her retirement. When she came to me, she explained she would be retiring from a major Aerospace company in about 18 months (the department was closing) and she would receive an amazing benefit package. The problem was, she couldn't see herself RETIRED! The word to her just seemed final or over. She went on to express that all she knew was her work and had recently gotten her PhD. However, the education was to benefit and elevate her in her field on her job.

The feeling of not knowing next steps was so foreign to her. From the outside it looked perfect; she was educated, retired, and in excellent health; however, unsure of the next steps…

Here's what I shared with her:

> *Dear "This is so Foreign to me,"*
>
> *Congratulations! I am so glad you are allowing me to assist you in this* ***ReInvention*** *and Discovery. Since we have already tackled the income questions and know that won't be an issue for you once you enter into retirement, let's talk about YOU. While you may be in unfamiliar territory, let me assure you, You got this!*
>
> *Let's go back to when you graduated from high school—yea, high school. You see, back then you were facing forward, looking life in the face with limited responsibilities and nothing but opportunities ahead. Fast forward, and you are here again. This time with more life experience that can add to MORE SECURE outcomes. When you graduate from high school, you're not jaded, you're hopeful, and still have the power of imagination. So, here's a question, what would you do if money was no object and time had no bearing on outcome?*

Just as I asked my client who had the opportunity forced upon her in this new place, we all find ourselves in foreign places we have never seen; like a Pandemic that took us all by surprise. Maybe a few imagination tips would be good for you too.

1. In the style of writing called "free form," write out every dream, idea, wish, and plan you ever had.

2. Mark off with a star all the ones you think you can achieve.

3. Make a plan for which one you're going to go after first and don't share the selection with anyone other-then someone who will encourage you.

4. Believe you can, focus, and MOVE.

Journal the Journey

Matthew 17:20

Matthew 17:20

Matthew 17:20

Where the path leads or Lead, and the path will develop

This week I was asked a question; as a corporate recruiter, it's a question I personally asked for years to candidates I offered employment to. The question was to design the life you see for yourself in three years. In other words, where do you see yourself in next three years?

I had never felt any concern regarding that question before, but for some reason, this time, it stumped me, and I assigned such a level of gravity to it. In the past, when asked, I could rattle off my 2-year, 5-year, and 10-year plans as easy as breathing, but on this day, my mind swirled with mental chatter.

As a woman of a certain age, wife, and mother extraordinaire, the question now has so many factors to be considered, how will my decisions affect my future personally and those around me who depend on me?

As a professional financial consultant, my main tool of choice is the ability to help my clients dream and picture where they want to be in the future. My job is in helping them plan the steps to get there. So, why was it so hard for me to give the answer, and implement the tool to my own dream plan?

Could it be, perhaps like you, I now put my family ahead of myself in that role as ***mom***? And in that role, chose the selfless sacrifice of $150 towards the college fund opposed to the $150 steal of a lifetime (cute, butter soft leather, tailored, zip front "Theory" blazer at Nordstrom — yes it was that cute, a perfect fit medium, I already had the stark white button down, black pencil skirt, and open-toed stiletto from my closet, already picked out) to be responsible and not seem as selfish.

Does this question also stump you, or have you been resilient and steadfast in your reverent pursuit of your dreams, withstanding the sway of life events and their impact on your dream plan? For those of us who have altered our dream plan, either by circumstance, situation, or design, how do we **reclaim** and **reload** it back into our path without feeling guilty or selfish, but empowered as leading?

If you remember, **ReLoad** means to start again, redo with a firm foundation. For some, you may feel your personal economy impacted your dream; for others it may be a change in title from single to married, married to single, or children at home to empty nesters.

No matter the reason, we have to make a choice to **ReLoad** our dream plan. Accept and revel in the new economic status or title change, acknowledging that the path is only as clear and as wide as the dream that manifests it, for the dream must be the unmovable anchor.

Conversations with Christyna

I was speaking to a young lady who had moved to North Carolina from New York. We were speaking about how she felt brand NEW, like she could do anything because there was so much land and she hadn't been out of New York, EVER. She wanted to speak about purchasing a condo and found that the prices in North Carolina were much lower than her RENT in New York. She was a new graduate and had just secured her first job (adult job). She wanted to know would it be good to get a 15-year mortgage or a 30 year, because what she had been paying for RENT equaled the amount of the 15-year mortgage for the condo she was looking at.

Dear Miss 15 yr. vs 30 yr.

I *absolutely love the place you find yourself. Can you say OPTIONS? Wow… where do I begin. I would like to ask you 1st, if you entered the 30-year contract, what could you see yourself doing with the difference (extra money), since you can handle the 15-year payment which would be a little more?*

Second, will there be a pre-payment penalty if you take the lower payment of the 30 year and double them, thus paying the property off sooner and having a reserve should you need if things got tight?

There is so much possibility here… Did I say HOW PROUD of you I am that you put yourself in position to have options, choices, trail, paths? Well, I truly am. So, let me say this Miss 15 yr. vs. 30 yr.:

1. *Check the fine print.*
2. *Do a Gut check (what looks good on paper doesn't always address all that is required).*
3. *Get excited.*
4. *Make a choice.*

Journal the Journey

Remember, brickless paths help us develop fortitude and vision for our comeback.

Now, let me hear you loud, bold, and empowered, where do you see yourself in the next three years?

Mark 9:23

Mark 9:23

Mark 9:23

Dorothy was distracted, what about you!

A friend sent me a text asking, out of true and sincere concern, if I was okay. They notice I had transformed (in a physical appearance) so much so that they wanted to make sure I wasn't sick. I thought about the sincerity and took a look at myself and acknowledged its significance. I thought about how I've been so caught up in my day-to-day grind, and likened it to a tornado of life, distracted by my own personal ***Toto***. The significance of my Toto's (distractions) had me so wrapped up I hadn't noticed my own transformation.

If you remember, it was that cold winter night that Dorothy went to take out the trash, just as Toto dashed out the door into the storm. Like a good caretaker, Dorothy left her primary task and ran after Toto. She was so distracted by her desire to make sure Toto was safe, she put herself in harm's way.

Which brings me to ask, *what's your Toto?* What tasks or things of significance in your life have you found yourself distracted by? What tornadoes have you been caught up in because your Toto ran out the door?

As a woman, we are excellent at multitasking, caregiving, and caretaking, but at what cost? Your Toto may be working instead of going back to school to increase your income, or forgoing work (income) to care for children, a parent, or a spouse. Your Toto could be Fear — False Evidence, Appearing Real — keeping you paralyzed in a rut. Were you supposed to have that vacation home but spent the extra monthly income on Saint John's knits—Toto? Were you supposed to retire last year but wanted a new car, so now you're working an extra 2 years—Toto? Or perhaps like mine, your Toto is not facing the truth that a tornado is what you're in and regardless of being distracted by running after your Toto, transformation is still happening.

Totos are anything that distracts us from keeping the main thing the *main thing.* Dorothy was so distracted; she couldn't see the transformative tornado that was heading her way. Remember, all it takes is realization to allow transformative moments to be **Realized**.

Journal the Journey

What transformative something have you not seen due to your distracting Toto? Identify the Toto or Totos in your life. Write out your goals, especially those you forgot, said would never happen, or gave up on. Cross reference and determine if a Toto has kept you from accomplishing your goals.

Proverbs 4:25

DOROTHY WAS DISTRACTED, WHAT ABOUT YOU?

Proverbs 4:25

DOROTHY WAS DISTRACTED, WHAT ABOUT YOU?

Proverbs 4:25

OMG! Relax, relate, release. I keep telling myself! I know I'm on the verge of greatness, but I feel this uneasy pull to stay right here reveling in the familiar. Does that sound like a tape you played yourself? Do you have a gnawing inside that's calling you to a place of unfamiliarity, however, if you just surrender to it, you will find great things await you?

The reality of seeking personal greatness is it takes an action; an action we don't always want to give in to—Movement. Walking the road to your personal greatness can be lonely, uncomfortable, and reflective.

Keeping true to the theme of the Wizard of Oz, the main character Dorothy (or you) had to step up and tell herself she could do it. Putting one foot in front of the other, she moved forward into the things of the unknown and pressing towards the mythical city where she would find the All-Mighty Wizard; however, she found something better along the way. She found her courage, heart, and brain. Her best!

Conversations with Christyna

The year is 2020 and will forever be known as the Pandemic year; I wanted to speak directly to you No matter when or what year you are taking this journey.

I've been thinking, we have ALL journeyed together into unchartered territory; we have made sourdough bread, have caught up on our Netflix play list, learned new hobbies, and have dealt with fear, the what-ifs and uneasiness of the unknown!

We have ALL entered into new realms by force!

All of our forward movement will be based on the COVID-19 Vaccine, which has caused me to wonder, when in my life have I been halted, waiting for a "vaccine," solution, or a hard break to start again into something that is totally different from what I had or had known. Here are my thoughts:

> *Dear CWC,*
>
> *WOW, I know exactly where I stand. I have actually stood paralyzed in place before. By all accounts, I looked like I was moving with the flow of the situation and doing a good job of it. That was from the outside, while inside I was crumbling. My*

Paralyzation, or "Pandemic," was my shame for divorcing my husband.

You see, they called us the Huxtables (after the characters from the famous Cosby show of the 90s) and everything was humming along, until I realized things were more serious than I knew. Perhaps like you when the shutdown happened in 2020; you felt like it would be for a few weeks and kept doing what you were doing until you found out it was more serious than your capacity was ready for.

Does that sound familiar? Well, as I said, I've been there. Here is what I'd like you to consider and maybe it will assist you:

1. BE ok with NOT being OK!
2. Find your friendship superpower and TAP INTO IT (meaning plug into your friendship circle, don't avoid them, let them LOVE on you).
3. LOVE ON YOURSELF UNAPOLOGETICALLY without any need of approval (read, write, hike, yoga, church, love, travel).
4. PLAN your next steps (without limits).

Journal the Journey

What will you find if you give your best another chance? Tell yourself. I can, I will, I must!

Habakkuk 2:2

CAN YOU SEE THE CITY FROM THERE?

Habakkuk 2:2

CAN YOU SEE THE CITY FROM THERE?

Habakkuk 2:2

You're the Wizard!

Smiles abound, the doors open, a loud baritone voice says, "Enter!" You walk towards the curtain, pull it back expecting to see a stately figure, instead, you see a mirror! Reflecting from the mirror is a face that looks familiar, but you can't make it out. You step closer, using your hand to wipe away the film, and **Realize** staring back at you is somebody that you used to know.

The You that You Used to Know!

I've been reflecting and **ReLoading** myself with the help of audio coaching. Some of the things I've noticed sparking back up inside of me have been my ambition, my drive, and my determination. That feeling that I can achieve anything.

Do you remember having that? That magic, that ability to speak it and be it, and what you wanted showed up? Do you remember when the magic left, or when you gave it away? What did it feel like? A better question—*what does it feel like now?*

Dorothy, her brain, heart, and courage pulled the curtain back and saw a small shriveled little man who called himself the wizard. If you remember, the wizard had the ability to grant anything to those who met him and asked. Let's really think about this… The little man, from the same place where Dorothy came from, was the grantor? Isn't it funny how we give our hopes, ideas, and dreams to others who we believe have more power or influence than we do? Why do we believe more in the power of others than we do in our own? What if you and I are the grantee and the grantor all in one? The Mythical All-Powerful Wizard!

As the wizard, you need a goal, something to help you focus your mind and efforts to pull you through when the road gets tough. No matter if it's physical, financial, or relational, two constants must always be present. A *high Goal* and a *high Standard*. Also, there must be *Belief*. Along the way you may attract a mentor or coach who's been there and done that approach can help you remember or guide you back to YOU!

Setbacks, changes, and life choices can sometimes fog or shield our view, but with a little **Realization**, what was old can be made new, igniting the flame of your imagination and fueling your inner Wizard.

So now, look into the mirror a little harder and see the image shaping—look familiar?

It's you, the wizard!

Journal the Journey

Philippians 4:13

Philippians 4:13

Philippians 4:13

You killed My sister!

It was the death of the sister that forced the movement of Dorothy on to the path. But that's too obvious. So how about this… She killed what was perceived and labeled as *bad* and was given the *good* out of it—The Slippers!

What if financial setbacks, fractured relationships, and slain goals were all simply purging and purification for the good; the revealing of the Ruby or Silver Slippers (whichever version you like, the Wizard of Oz or the Wiz)?

Consider this, the East sister dies at the start of the movie (or Dorothy's new life), and at the end of the movie the sister of the West dies (the song "Can You Feel a Brand New Day" blast in the background—Wiz version). Are you thinking what I'm thinking? Can you see where I'm going here?

If you recall, there was the Wicked Witch of the West and the Wicked Witch of the East (the witch of the east dies). No matter where you are on this planet that we call earth, the sun rises from the East and sets in the West. The East is in the past and the West is your future; the middle is the journey.

In order to make the most of this, she had to relax, relate, and release, and move. For you and I, I see it as we have to **Realize, ReLearn, ReLoad** to move!

So, let's take a small step forward, what will you do with your day after the East of the morning is dead!

Conversations with Christyna

This isn't unique to 2020, but since this book was bridged in that year and I fancy myself a transition specialist, I wanted to speak directly to you; whether you are a graduate from high school wondering where the path will lead since NOTHING is nor was normal, a business owner that now has no business, a parent whose children boomeranged and came home to stay and are now free thinking adults in your house, or someone who is simply in a FORCED TRANSITION.

Here is my invitation to you:

Find something to do that you ENJOY and feel is WORTH doing. If there is anything the Pandemic taught us, it is LIFE is worth LIVING and there is still so much LIVING to do. LIVE on your own terms. Do you know how many lawyers I know who hated every moment of their career and got the degree only for glamor of the title, i.e., parent, status, security?

Security is what you make it. A job is not security, money is not security. Those are instruments that assist in CREATING security. There are so many stories of super successful people who took their own lives due to not being fulfilled. So many broken families, because a spouse only worked and never shared the things they were working for with the person they said they loved. Find your worth within YOURSELF and let the outside take care of itself.

1. Find your WHAT... What do you like; in fact, what do you LOVE.

2. Free your mind! Take time to just look up or look out. Free your mind, creativity, imagination.

3. BECOME, if you're not who you want to be, BECOME it. The forced move to online learning opened up so much.

4. ADD ADVENTURE to your life.

Journal the Journey

Romans 8:28

Romans 8:28

Romans 8:28

Send the Flying Monkeys!

I was speaking with a friend who shared how they were going through a very hard time with the dissolution of a relationship. It was interesting that the relationship was that of a business partnership, which had been four years in the making and two years in actual existence.

They expressed the most challenging part of the process was breaking down the financial obligations; the WHO is responsible for WHAT moving forward, because everything was still going to be needed, just now under individual business names. They were so stressed that they started getting upset saying they wish they could just scrap it and start over. Which got me thinking…

Couple–hood, no matter at what level, be it friendship, partnership, consultancy, or marriage, requires defined roles regarding our relationships and handling of money. You can't move into the quintessential couple–hood and achieve the goals of the address without the understanding that it takes a clear vision of money rolls to sustain it. Otherwise, frustration, stress, and flying monkeys will creep in or be summonsed.

A business colleague of mine, Kathleen, spoke of the couple–hood of marriage like this, "It's a strange, wonderful, and wild ride." Universally, it's the relationship that challenges us like no other. Sometimes it is predictable. Other times it has unexpected twists and turns, and money plays a big role in the journey.

Couples consciously and unconsciously decide how to spend and enjoy money, how to save and amass wealth, and how to use money to exert power and control in the relationship. Some partners fight about money, others worry about it. Some couples joined forces and create a strong financial and emotional bond, while others never seem to trust each other financially.

When we undergo the task of a partnership, we do it in good faith, not believing that in latter days, for whatever reason, a dissolution can happen, be it death, divorce, or taxman. That out of lack of knowledge, we will be summoning the flying monkeys to come do our bidding.

So, to avoid this misstep, I suggest taking a moment to take your financial temperature, realize where your affairs reside in their current state, then **ReLearn** (with whoever you are in the couple–hood with) how to establish clear money roles. I use a tool in my business called a Financial Survey.

This helps to provide perspective and insight. Feel free to contact me if you believe you are blind in this area; otherwise, someone will be saying, send in the flying monkeys, and we don't want that!

Conversations with Christyna

I had a conversation with a referral recently. He was referred to me from a friend who is also my business partner. I make the distinction purposefully, because sometimes business should simply be that—BUSINESS. He called and shared that he was looking for financial assistance and advice. The last person he spoke to directed him in a way he felt wasn't cool. I told him I would be happy to listen and see if it was a good fit and asked what his issue was… and he shared this.

"I am a 30-year-old single man living in Los Angeles. I am an entrepreneur who has more money than I know what to do with."

I must tell you; I love confidence in a man. It is the sexiest thing on the planet, however, as a financial strategist and fiduciary, I always LISTEN to reframe, so I asked him, "What is too much money?"

He said, "I'm just on the edge of 6 figures."

Now this could go one of two ways... Here is what I shared with him:

Dear More Money than I know what to do with, I am so glad that in a year such as what we have experienced in 2020, you are able to declare with confidence, I MAKE MONEY. For so many, income has simply been OUT GO, so you are so, so lucky. When I asked how much you made, you weren't sure; you said you make sporadically as an entrepreneur, but your bills total to $3,000 per month and you cover those easily. My suggestion before we enter into any further conversation is let's take the next 90 days and you keep every receipt, every bank statement, and every PayPal or square document and we will come back and see exactly what the AVERAGE monthly Income is, and what the Out Go is, so we can see exactly what you KEEP.

Yes, KEEP! You see, our culture is so wrapped up in what we have, and what we make fuels the illusion of having; however, the name of the game is in the KEEP. Rich is brash and flashy; Wealth is silent and influential. So, which would you want me to call you, Rich or Wealthy, Mr. More than I know what to do with?

Here are some steps to ensure you are on the path to wealth:

1. Make all transactions using a card for the next 90 days and limit the cash transactions.
2. Use your business card for all business transactions.
3. With each transaction, on each card, separate out the fluff from the necessity.
4. Strip out the IN Come from the OUT GO.
5. Let the game begin, now that you know what you MAKE and what you KEEP.

Journal the Journey

Psalm 46:1

Psalm 46:1

Psalm 46:1

we represent... The Lollipop Guild

So, this past Saturday, like most of you, I went to do my errands, chores, and add to the ever expanding To Do List. One of my destinations on the to do list was a birthday party at an enclosed jungle gym with bounce house, zip line, table tennis, and air hockey; a child's play haven with not a care in the world—except how many times can I go down a blow-up slide?

I've been to this gym many times for family fun nights, but never for a birthday party. They move all the children onto a rug and ask, "Are you all ready to have fun?" By the way, the sign on the wall says, "Fun is mandatory!" With jubilant voices all in unison, an ear piercing Yes! resounded. And poof, the magic fun door opened.

I turned to another parent who had a baby Bjorn strapped to the front of her and asked, "Do you wish adult life offered that fun question?"

And that got me to—Wait for it—Thinking! When our main character dropped into Oz, she was greeted by singing munchkins of The Lollipop Guild, who welcomed her to this *new land* with a song!

What if every challenge the new day brought came after a morning serenade or a call to mandatory fun? How do you believe you would respond? What would that small greeting or call empower you to *Do* differently, *Think* differently, or *See* differently in your personal circumstances? What would your jubilant response be to the challenges of life? Yes! I can't, or maybe next time.

So back to the magic fun door opening at the kids' party, where mandatory fun is required; what if we adults **ReLearned** how to have fun and renamed life's challenges as *Adult Fun*? What song are you downloading to your playlist as your morning wake up fun song?

Life is Complicated
-that's what makes it
Fun!

Nehemiah 8:10

Journal the Journey

Nehemiah 8:10

Nehemiah 8:10

Nehemiah 8:10

I live in Southern California, where the term overcast becomes a daily event from April through July. It's the time of the year where the prediction of sun only comes after the morning overcast has melted away. The closer you are to the coastline or beaches, the longer it takes to see the sun breaking through. It's interesting to me how we become familiar with the foggy overcast of the season, so much so that it is expected; it's our normal.

Ponder this basic question: Has there been foggy overcast seasons in your life, where you knew later in the day, the sun was predicted to breakthrough; but, in the midst of the fog, you felt closed in and couldn't see the rays of light breaking through?

Our main character landed in an unfamiliar place, with impaired vision and lost bearings. Perspective in the fog is hard to gauge, even with knowing the bright rays of sun is on its way. Sometimes it's hard to be on the road to your goal (your comeback) when the foggy overcast comes.

It causes questioning and doubt; however, if we have our feet firmly on the road toward our goal when that foggy overcast season rolls in, we can be like the joggers on the beach and have our shorts and sunglasses on with no apparent sun.

With your sunglasses on, stay the course towards your goal. Along the way you'll find that rays of the sun will breakthrough and reveal where you've been walking was the actual path to your comeback. And don't worry, I'll walk with you.

Calling All Bricklayers...

Grab your heels, throw on your power song, work on your stance, shoulders back, head high—Now Strut! Remember, if you feel good, youAreGood!

Journal the Journey

Acts 9:18

Acts 9:18

Acts 9:18

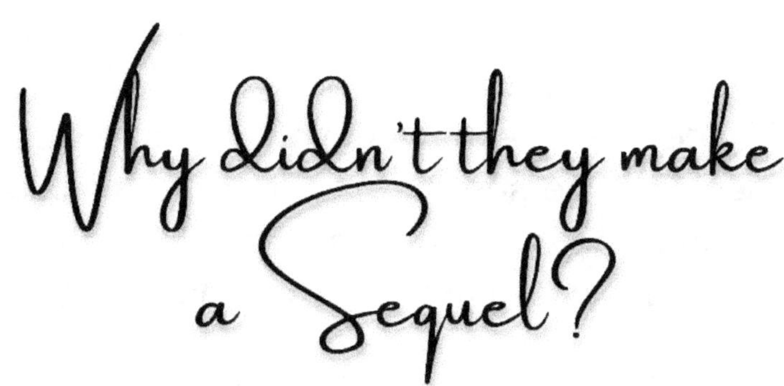

Have you ever noticed when you watch some movies, they leave you wondering what happened later? Wishing they would make a sequel to let you know how the situation changed or if the characters survived, fell in love, got the bad guy, etc.?

Isn't that always the case, when something is good, we want more of it; kind of like we desire completion. If you are like me that desire doesn't always translate to laundry, cleaning out the closet, or washing dishes; those seem to never be complete.

In 2013, I noticed it shaped into being the year for movie sequels. I'm a big movie buff, and during that summer all the sequels were coming out; GI Joe, Iron Man 3, The Hangover 3, Grownups 2, Despicable Me 2, Smurfs 2, Star Trek 2, and so on (and again in 2019 with all the TV Reboots). But isn't it funny how movies can be critically deemed awful, yet be popular enough to get a studio to invest in creating another one, a sequel?

Which causes me to pose this question to you: *Is it possible to have a personal sequel?* 2012 was a very Topsy Turvy year for me personally. The mountain was a little steeper than it appeared, yet I continued to climb. For some of us, we see the height of the mountain as insurmountable or the financial set back too deep a hole to get out of; but what if there was a sequel to it?

A sequel is a redo. A sequel usually has the same characters but now in new settings and with new storylines. It's a continuation of the first movie.

If you recall, **ReLearning** is to come to know or know how, and **ReLoading** is to make ready for firming. Applying these two definitions to your personal sequel basically means ***It Ain't Over!*** Only part of the movie has ended, but the sequel is in production. Sometimes the sequel is bigger and introduces new characters and provides a deeper understanding of the original cast!

So, no matter what it looks like now, how bad or good, how miserably the idea failed, or how many thousands less you have in your account, the story is not over. You are popular enough to invest in your own sequel. Be the hero or heroine, love interest, or villain in your own sequel.

Plans:

If you want something to happen in your life you have to make room for it!

Planning is a matter of probabilities, which means that sometimes your plans will turn out and sometimes they won't. You can save yourself a lot of stress by realizing that sooner rather than later.

A little hint: it is ok for plans to cover many time spans, as short as an hour and as far out as 20 years. Create a pathway for your dreams to travel and you just follow.

Journal the Journey

2 Corinthians 5:17

2 Corinthians 5:17

2 Corinthians 5:17

2 Corinthians 5:17

You knew I couldn't leave you without a challenge—Right?

For this I had to call in the stage play "Wicked." For those of you who are not familiar with the story, it is about the friendship of Glenda (the Good Witch) and Elphaba (the Wicked Witch of the West), before Dorothy dropped in.

Elphaba Realizes that she wanted more and was finally okay with being different. She wanted to explore her newfound ambitions and freedom outside of Oz, and she announces her newfound power in the magnificent song "Defying Gravity."

> *"Something has changed within me; something is not the same—I'm threw with playing by the rules of someone else's game…"*

At that moment, she found her voice. She used her courage and freed her heart to speak her truth and unapologetically put herself first!

As she says, *"I think I'll try defying gravity…"*

Then comes the famous line belting out of Idina Menzel's mouth,

> *"And if you dare to find me, look to the western sky…"*

She rises, seeming to float, and she realized she is now weightless—Defying Gravity.

So, Bricklayers…

I invite you to release your Roar and let the world know you choose to live Free:

Without self-imposed limits **LIMITLESS**

With a clear Direction **VISION**

With Your first choices **FREEDOM**

I am so glad you took this journey with me, and I will look to the West and hope to see you in all of your greatness, living the life you have created, celebrating yourself to the fullest, smiling, laughing, and flying, living your best life on your own terms.

Please, when it gets overwhelming, drop me a line and know I am always there, walking that road with you.

christynawithay@gmail.com
Convowithc.com.

An old Baptist song says,

"One step, all I have to do is take one step and He will do the rest..."

Lao-tzu said,

"A journey of 1000 miles begins with one step..."

CWC says,

"Sometimes, Belief in yourself is required..."

Journal the Journey

Now that you have found your heart, courage, voice, and brain and have journeyed through your self-discovery. How will you Defy Gravity?

Ephesians 3:20

Ephesians 3:20

Wait, Dont go just yet!

I know I shared in the beginning of this journey I have been in Financial Services and I am sure you may have wondered where the financial advice was.

Well, just as I asked in "Why didn't they make a Sequel?" I wanted to let you know I Will Be!

You see, Money Matters are actually Mental Matters. It is all in where value is placed and it is my desire to share tips and thoughts in the second installment, "Financial Stepping Stones, The Journey to a Lifestyle."

See you when we will be uncovering Gemstones…

www.ingramcontent.com/pod-product-compliance
Lightning Source LLC
LaVergne TN
LVHW010104110826
845155LV00028B/468

9781948085540